Action Alphabet

by Marty Neumeier and Byron Glaser

Greenwillow Books, New York

Library of Congress
Cataloging in Publication Data.
Neumeier, Marty.
Action Alphabet.
Summary: The letters of the alphabet
appear as parts of pictures repre-
senting sample words, such as a drip
formed by a D coming out of a faucet
and a vampire with V's for fangs.
1. English language—Alphabet—
Juvenile literature.
I. Glaser, Byron.   II. Title.
PE1155.N48   1985   [E]   84-25322
ISBN 0-688-05703-9
ISBN 0-688-05704-7 (lib. bdg.)

Aa : Acrobat

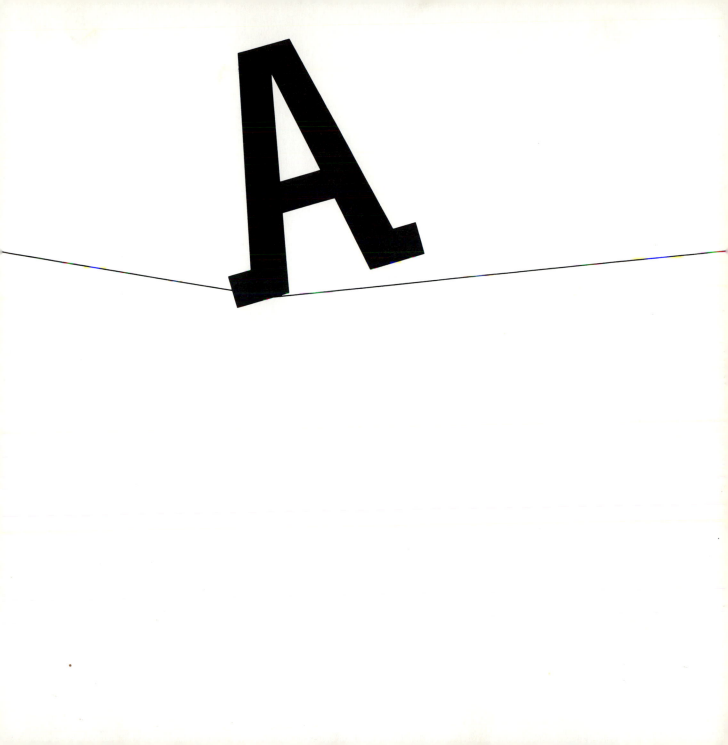

Bb : Big

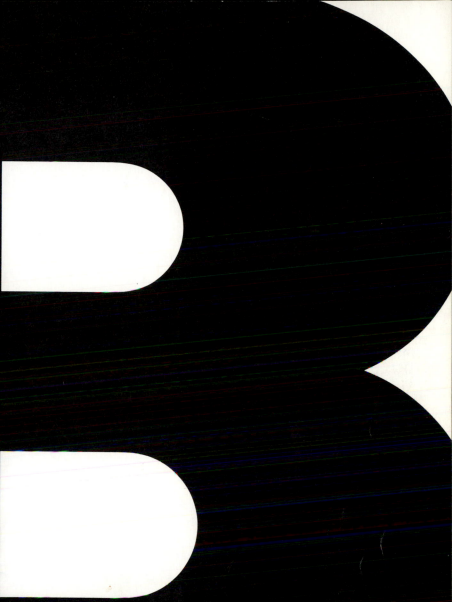

Cc : Crack

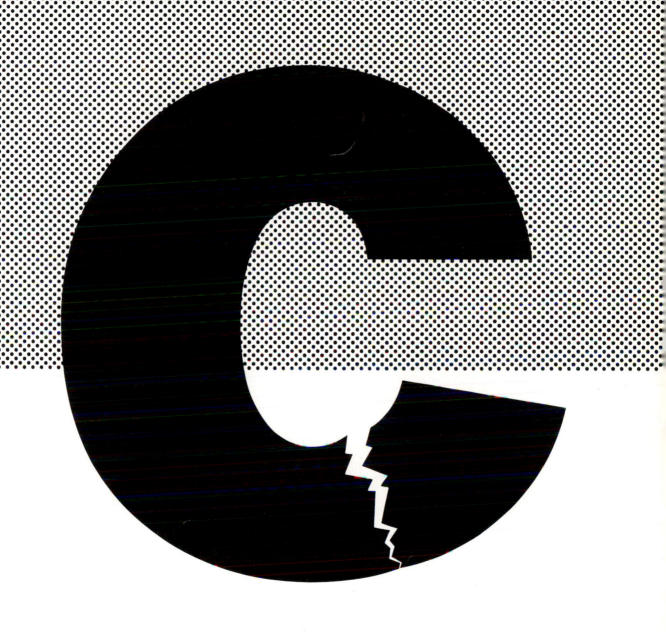

Dd : Drip

Ee : Eat

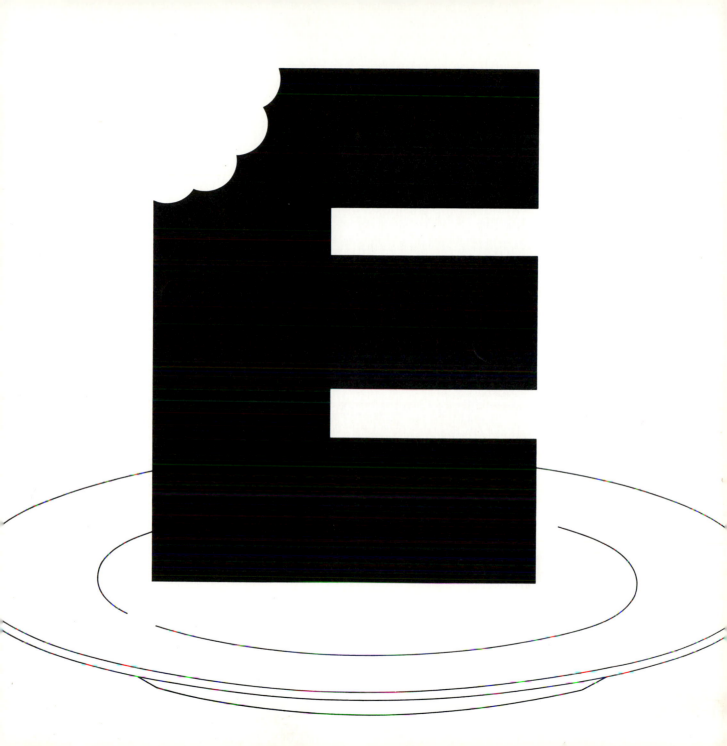

Ff : Fall

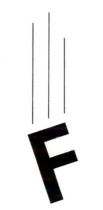

Gg : Gone

Hh : Hang

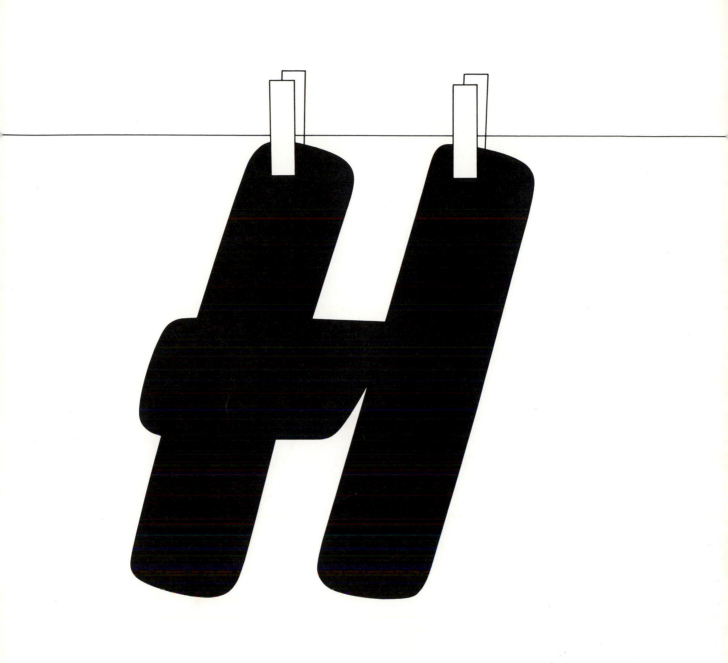

Ii : Ice Skate

Jj : Jump

Kk : Kite

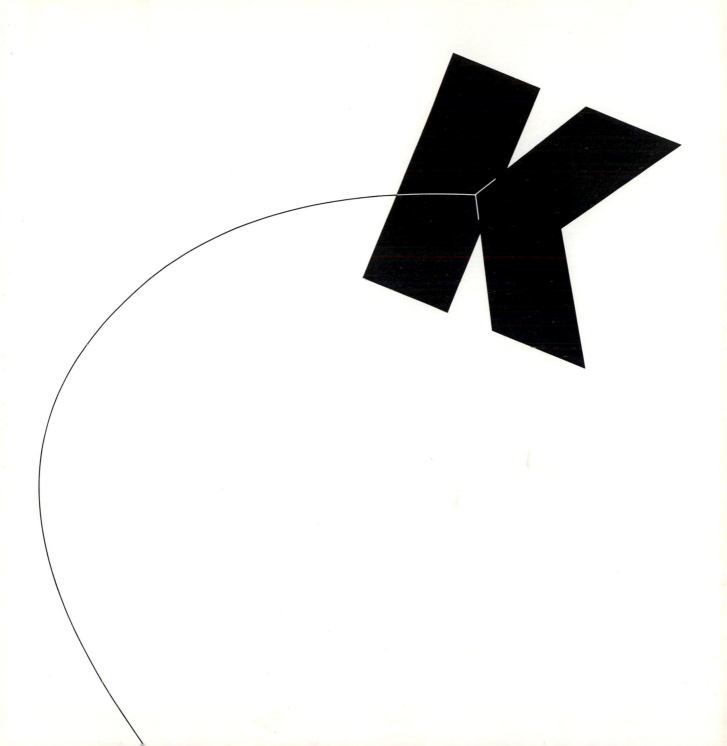

Ll : Letter

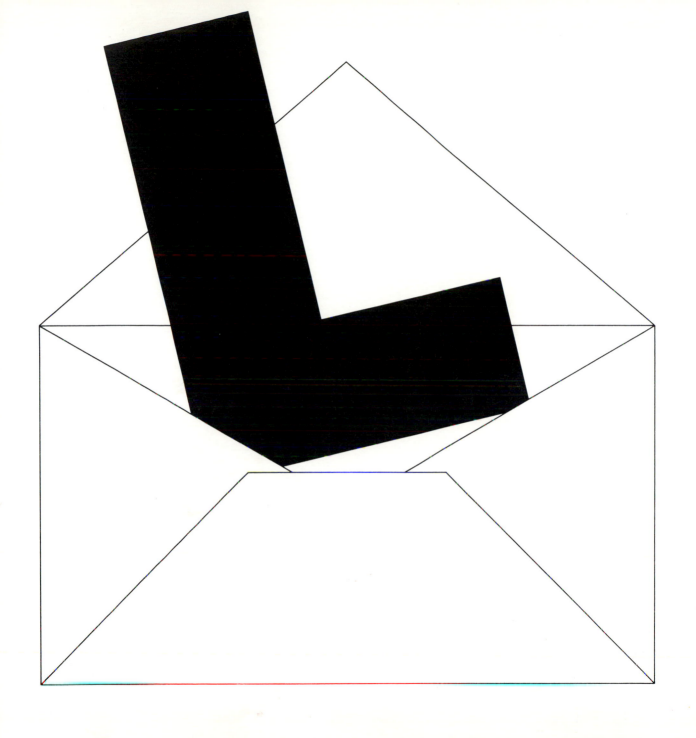

Mm : Mistake

Nn : Net

Oo : Orbit

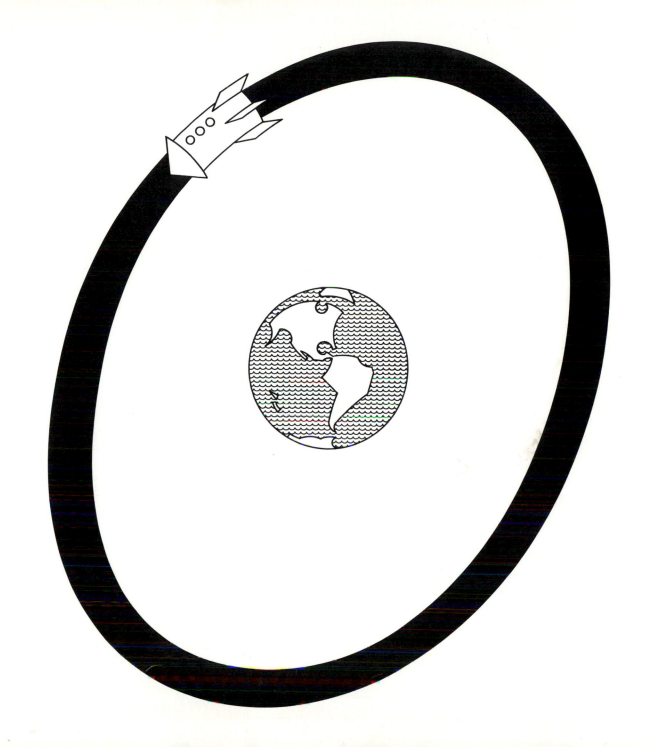

Pp : Piano

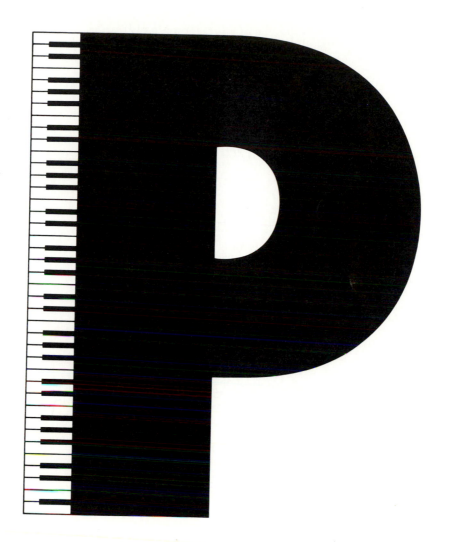

Qq : Quick

Rr : Rain

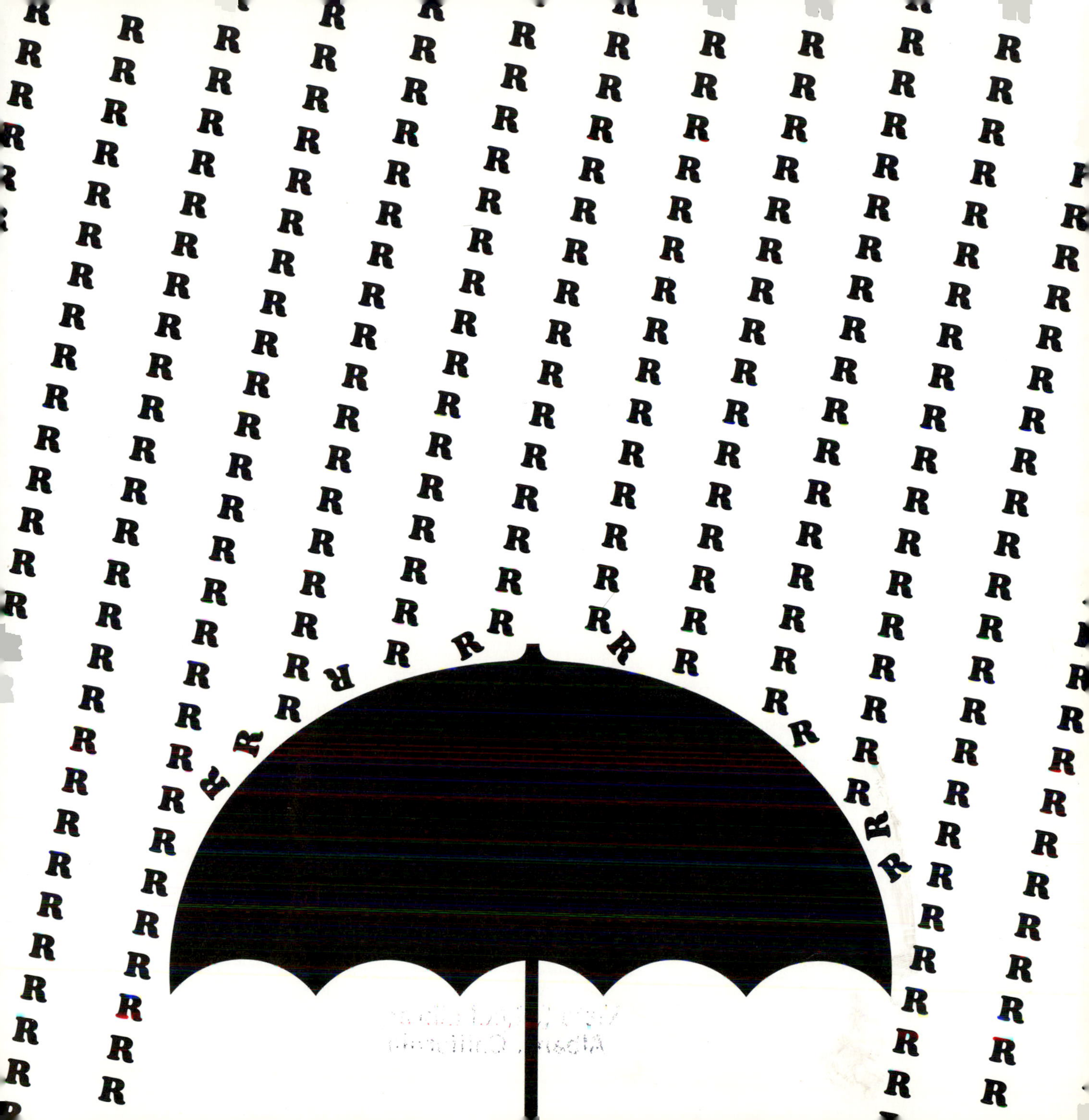

Ss : Small

SsSS

Tt : Twist

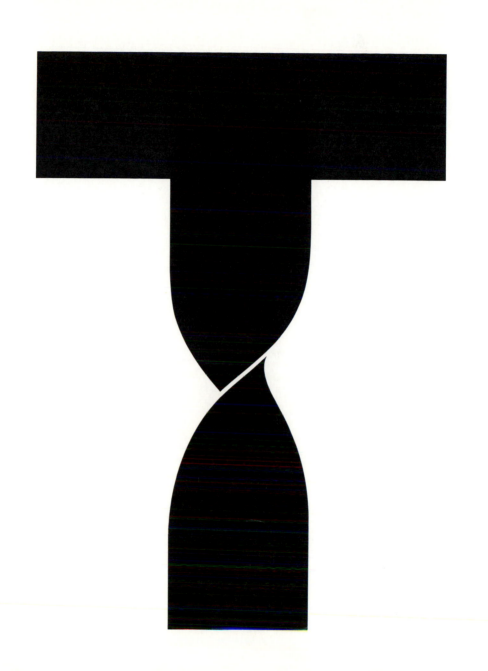

Uu : Up

U

rst vwx

Vv : Vampire

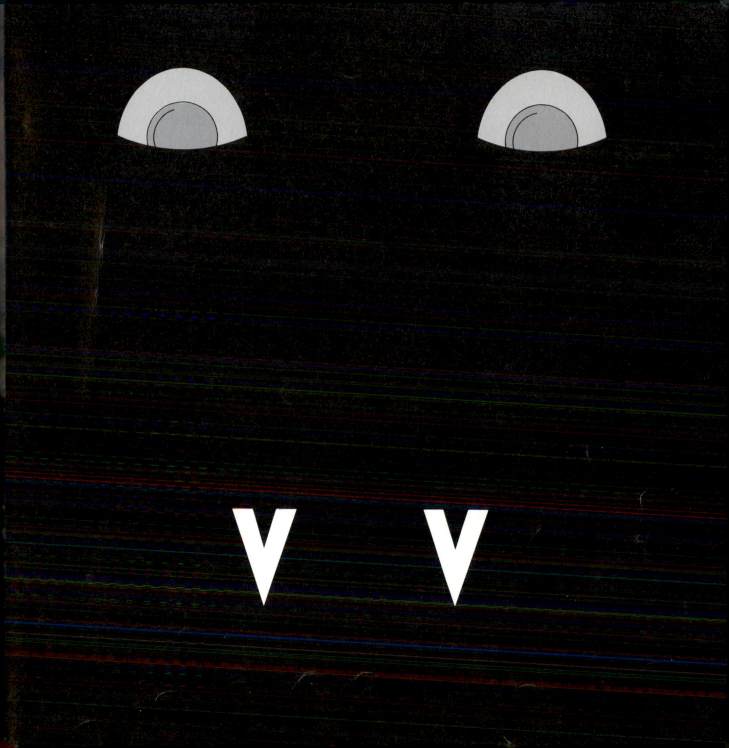

Ww : Walk

Xx : X-ray

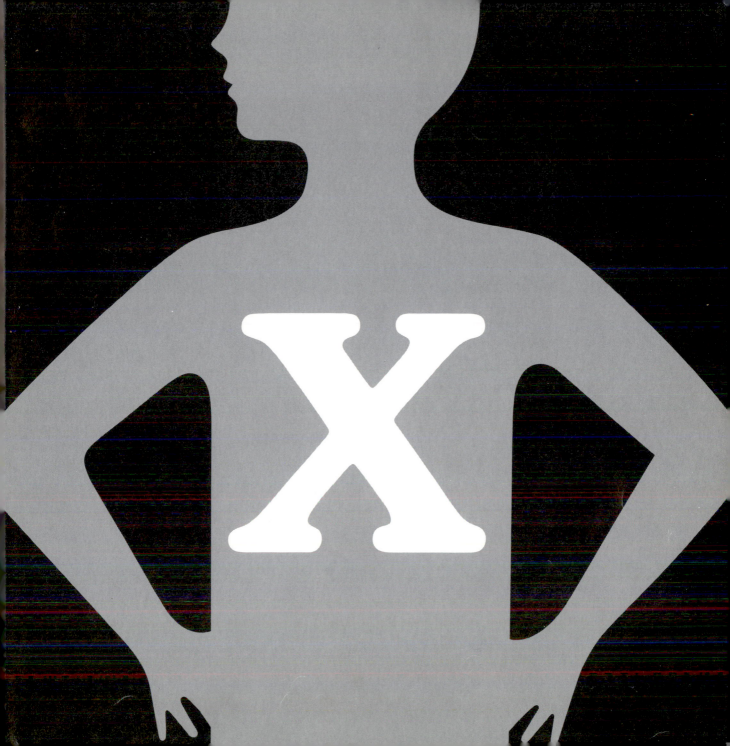

Yy : Yell

Zz : Zigzag

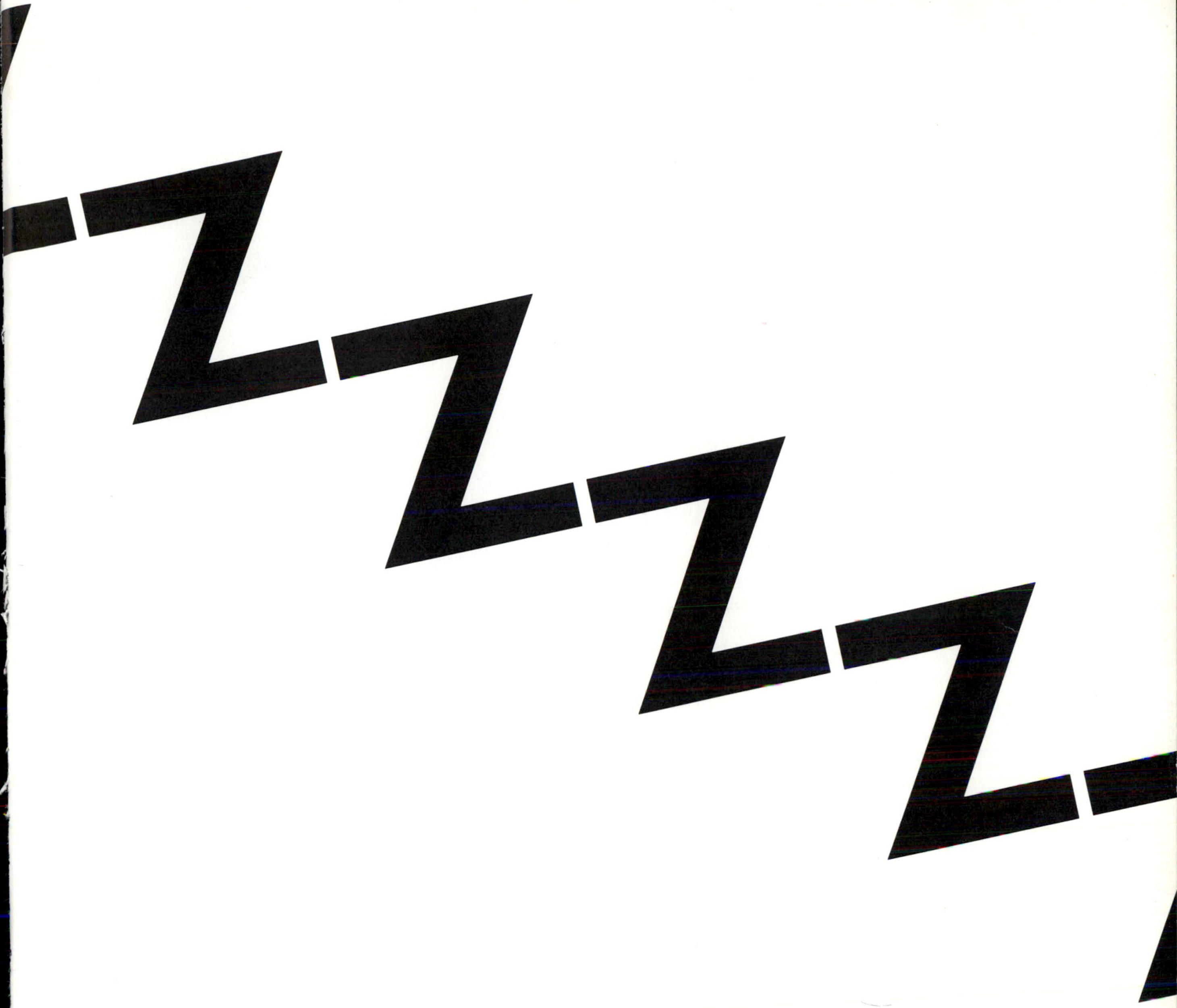

Marty Neumeier and Byron Glaser, both graphic designers, created the *Action Alphabet* as a studio project of the Neumeier Design Team. Since 1973 the studio has received hundreds of design honors, including a number of gold medals and several international exhibitions. Byron Glaser now works as a graphic designer in New York, while Marty Neumeier continues to operate the Neumeier Design Team near San Francisco.